BANGOR

A Pictorial History
(Volume 2)

by

John Cowell

First published in 1997

ISBN 0 9518592 3 4

PREFACE

THIS BOOK is intended to complement the first volume of *Bangor – a Pictorial History*, published in 1994, and therefore has much the same format. Its purpose is to recapture the nostalgia of an age which has gone for ever but should never be forgotten. Older readers will recognise many of the views and, perhaps, some of the personalities in the photographs, but much of the book will be unfamiliar to the younger generation. One hopes, however, that they will appreciate the changes which took place in the physical appearance of Bangor, as well as in all aspects of town life, during the first half of the twentieth century.

Facts have been derived, wherever possible, from contemporary sources. These include local newspapers and periodicals, business directories, guide books, council minute books, Census Returns and various manuscript collections. A number of published works of local interest have also been consulted, a list of which appears at the end of Volume 1. Any errors of fact arising from the misinterpretation of sources are entirely mine.

Money is expressed in its original pounds, shillings and pence, leaving the reader to make the conversion on the basis of 12d = 5p.

I acknowledge with profound gratitude the assistance received from Mr Tomos Roberts, the Archivist of the University of Wales, Bangor, who cheerfully gave me a great deal of help in locating the relevant manuscripts in his care, and to Miss Diana Clarke for her courteous assistance. I am also grateful to the staff of the County Record Office, Caernarfon, and the Post Office Archives in London; to Dr Peter Ellis Jones for allowing me to quote from his book *Bangor 1883-1983, a Study in Municipal Government*; to Mr Richard Williams for his help in locating the sources of a number of old photographs; to Mr David Roberts for expertly reproducing many of the illustrations; to Mrs Val Kenyon for her meticulous care in typesetting; and to countless other people who willingly supplied information not found elsewhere.

I am especially grateful to the following for the loan of original photographs and for their kindness in allowing me to reproduce them in the book: Mrs Pat Benneyworth, pages 9, 40, 41, 56, 74, 76, 92, 104, 114; Mrs Lyn Bussey, pp. 25, 37, 46; Miss Dilys Jones, p.82; Mrs Eileen Owens, pp.49, 51, 62, 65; Mrs Phylis Parry, p.88; Miss Dilys Tharme, p.4; Miss Iris Williams, p.48; Mrs Nellie Williams, pp.78, 85; Mr Michael Day, p.34; Mr Dennis Edwards, p.54; Mr Seth Edwards, p.57; Mr Gwilym Hughes, pp.28, 90; Mr Peter Ellis Jones, p.53; Mr Brian Leavett, p.97; Mr John Nickels, p.58; Mr Norman Owen, pp.55, 106; Mr David Price, p.36; Mr Albert Talbot, p.8; Mr Ken Williams, pp.99, 100, 101; Bangor City Council, pp.21, 105.

Every effort has been made to trace the original owners of other photographs in my possession, but where this has not been possible I can only apologise for any unintentional breach of copyright.

Finally, I hope that this second volume will act as a permanent reminder of what Bangor was like in former days, and that it gives readers as much pleasure as I derived in compiling it.

Menai Bridge   *John Cowell*
October 1997

A typical postcard from the Edwardian era. This was the 'golden age' of postcards which led to an unstoppable craze for collecting, and during the years leading up to the First World War over 800 million cards were posted annually in Britain. Their popularity was helped by the cheap and efficient service provided by the Post Office when, even at the halfpenny rate, they could be guaranteed to reach their destination the next morning. In 1918 the postal rate was doubled to a penny, and thereafter the popularity of postcards declined sharply.

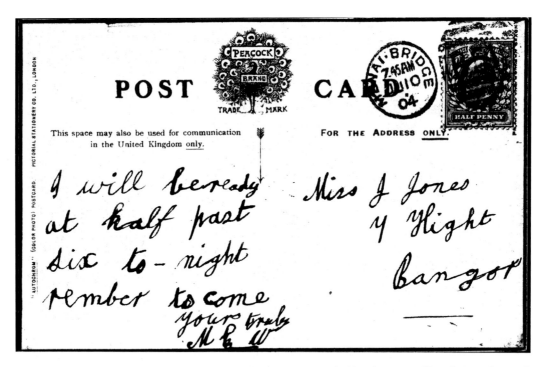

POST CARD

PEACOCK BRAND
TRADE MARK

This space may also be used for communication in the United Kingdom only.

FOR THE ADDRESS ONLY.

HALF PENNY

I will be ready at half past six to-night rember to come
your truly
M E W

Miss J Jones
4 Hight
Bangor

This postcard of 1904 epitomizes the splendid service provided by the Post Office during the peak of its performance. The writer posted the card in Menai Bridge early on the morning of 10th June, confident that it would arrive in Bangor later that same day. As there were four deliveries of mail each weekday in the town, the postcard would have reached Jennie Jones shortly after midday, in plenty of time for her to make arrangements to meet her friend that evening.

The outdoor staff of the Head Post Office in 1949. The postal rate for letters at this time was 2½d. It was subsequently raised to 3d in 1957 – only the fifth increase since the introduction of Uniform Penny Postage in 1840 – whereas in the last thirty years rates have increased no fewer than twenty-one times. In addition to the 'GPO' in Deiniol Road there were nine sub-offices in Bangor – Hirael, Glanadda, Ffriddoedd, Penrhosgarnedd, Upper Bangor, Maesgeirchen, Pendref, Garth and High Street. The last three have since closed.

The junction of High Street and Dean Street before the empty shop on the corner (No. 315) was demolished in 1935 as part of the council's road improvement scheme. The shop was formerly occupied by Thomas Lewis, grocer, who re-located his business next door. The re-development of the area was completed in 1939 with the building of 42 council houses in Dean Street and Well Street, together with the widening of both roads.

The County Theatre, Dean Street, in 1931. This was the former Tabernacle Calvinistic Methodist chapel which was used as a roller skating rink before being purchased by James Hare and converted into a 'handsome and commodious theatre', with seating for 800. It opened in September 1912 and provided drama, concerts, pantomimes and musical comedies before becoming a 'picture house' in 1918. Films at first were silent and accompanied by a pianist until the arrival of 'talkies' in 1929. By the late thirties cinema-going had become firmly established as a cheap and popular form of mass entertainment, with admission prices as low as 9d. During the Second World War the County Theatre was used extensively by the BBC Variety Department, which had been evacuated to Bangor, before reverting to a cinema after the BBC had returned to London in 1943.

Dean Street in flood in February 1929. Two inches of rain had fallen in less than an hour, causing the River Adda to overflow its banks and to flood houses in the low lying districts of Dean Street, Hirael and West End. The Adda was an open river for most of its length, and flooding became an ever present problem whenever heavy rain coincided with high tides. It was not until a flood prevention scheme was carried out in the early thirties that the nuisance was finally eradicated.

Improving the culverts of the River Adda at the bottom of Dean Street in 1931 as part of the city's flood prevention scheme. This included channelling most of the river underground, constructing larger flumes and installing a new outflow system at Hirael beach at a cost of £1,320. From Glynne Road to Beach Road the Adda remained an open river but its banks were raised by several feet in order to minimise the risk of flooding. It was finally culverted in 1960 in preparation for the building of the indoor swimming baths.

A fine animated view of the High Street on a postcard of the early 1900s, when children could play in the middle of the road safe in the knowledge that they would not be run over. The shops on the left are Humphreys & Parry, newsagents (No. 283), William Jones, hairdresser & tobacconist (285), J. Pickering, boot repairer & clog maker (287), the White Lion public house (289), D.G. Roberts, butcher (291), Edmund Gibbons, confectioner (293), Thomas Owen, saddler (295), and J. Thomas, draper, London House (297).

97376 HIGH STREET AND TOWN CLOCK, BANGOR, N. WALES

High Street from the opposite direction some twenty years later, but there is still no traffic to be seen. The physical appearance of this stretch of the High Street has changed considerably. The Woolworth store was built in 1939, new properties replaced the two shops on the right, while the large Masonic Hall was demolished in 1962 to make way for the Wellfield shopping centre. Note the prominent gas lamp outside Morton's shoe shop. This, along with all the city's street lights, was converted to electricity in 1925.

Brynhyfryd, a spacious house occupied by Dr J.H. Davies, a medical practitioner, before its demolition in 1939 to make way for the building of the Woolworth store. Brynhyfryd was part of the Wellfield Estate which extended from High Street to the Police Station. It was acquired by the City Council in 1951 with a view to building a new town hall on the site, but the scheme never materialised and the property was sold in 1962 for the construction of the Wellfield shopping complex.

An unidentified car owner and his passenger pose for the camera outside the offices of John Pritchard & Company, auctioneers and valuers, opposite the town clock, in 1920. The firm had been established in 1863 by Robert Pritchard, a former postmaster of Bangor, after his dismissal from the office 'for falsifying his stamp account'. His son gradually gained control of the business and it flourished for over a hundred years until it lost its identity in 1986.

A large crowd gathers outside the 'Old Bank' (now Lloyds) on 25th August 1883 to celebrate the granting of a civic charter to the city. This established Bangor as a municipal borough, governed by an elected council to replace the undemocratic Local Board of Health. This coincided with the welcome announcement that Bangor had been selected as the site for the new University College of North Wales. There is no town clock to be seen in the photograph as it was not erected until 1887.

Horse-drawn hackney carriages line up for fares alongside the cabmen's shelter hut in 1911. Whenever a fire occurred in Bangor these were among the first horses to be commandeered to pull the fire engine, which was then housed in the nearby town hall outbuildings. The newly-erected University College building, opened a few months earlier, can be seen in the background, with the probate office encircled by railings on the left.

HIGH STREET AND TOWN CLOCK, BANGOR, N.W.

There was a two-way system of traffic in the High Street when this postcard was written in 1947. Because of the inevitable congestion which this caused, a one-way flow down the street was put into operation in October of the following year. In 1953 parking restrictions were introduced, and partial pedestrianization followed in 1973. Note the milkman on his daily round in a horse-drawn cart. Prior to being sold in bottles, milk was supplied direct from the churn into the customer's jug by means of a measuring can.

HIGH STREET, BANGOR.

The Liverpool Arms, seen on the right of this 1950s postcard, was an inn of considerable importance during the first half of the nineteenth century, when the London-Holyhead mail coach and a number of public stagecoaches passed its doors each day. Sadly, the building was demolished in 1987. Nixon & Jarvis, Bangor's oldest stationer, stands on the opposite corner. Its imaginative and neatly-arranged window display always seemed to be full of interesting wares to tempt customers inside.

By 1910, when this postcard was written, multiple shops were beginning to make inroads into the High Street. But the small shopkeeper continued to survive by offering a personal service such as the delivery of goods, and more importantly, the granting of credit to trusted customers. Unlike today, where the High Street is dominated by national chain stores, in 1910 there were as many as 42 independent grocers in Bangor, 21 butchers, 33 drapers and outfitters, 23 bakers and confectioners, and 13 boot and shoemakers.

A view of the High Street from the opposite direction on a postcard written by a soldier stationed in Bangor in 1915, although the card was originally published some ten years earlier. It bears the message 'I will soon be going to the front where it is a bit livelier'. Even before the coming of motor transport there were reports of congestion in the High Street, with frequent complaints in the *North Wales Chronicle* that drapers' barrows, delivery wagons and milk carts were obstructing the highway during business hours.

The window display of the Central Book Mart at No. 202A High Street, opposite the Cathedral, appears to attract some interest on a summer's day in 1905. Williams & Company were well-known booksellers and stationers who also produced postcards of local views, but by 1910 the firm had ceased trading. Wartski's jewellery shop, formerly the Star Hotel, is situated next door at No. 202, while R.B. Watson's hairdressing saloon is at No. 204.

Cameron's fashionable gent's outfitting shop in Cathedral Buildings c.1890. Donald Cameron (1837-1915), the middle one of the three men in the photograph, was a native of Inverness who came to Bangor as a travelling draper before opening his shop in the High Street. He served as a Liberal member of the city council from 1884 and was elected mayor nine years later. He retired from business in 1912 and sold the shop to G.O. Griffith.

An early engraving published c.1840 by William Shone, a Bangor bookseller. The Cathedral, which was founded by Saint Deiniol in the sixth century, was almost entirely rebuilt and enlarged after the town is said to have been burnt in 1211, but suffered further damage during the Owain Glyndŵr rising of 1402. Its final reconstruction was completed by 1532. The road in front of the Cathedral was the city market place, then appropriately named Market Street, where a number of women can be seen selling their wares.

The Castle Hotel, one of the oldest inns in Bangor, on a postcard of 1906, showing a horse-drawn omnibus waiting to convey guests to the railway station. Formerly known as the Eagles, its name was changed to the Mitre in 1811, and ten years later it became the Castle Inn. Until its closure in 1989 the Castle was a high-class hotel, with forty bedrooms, a ballroom and a garage for a hundred cars. The building was demolished in 1996 to make way for the Littlewoods store.

Wartski's fashionable store gaily decorated for the 1953 Coronation. The premises were
opened by Isidore Wartski, a Polish Jew, who had taken over and expanded the business
established by his father in the late 1880s. The new store represented a transformation
in retailing, with its elegant surroundings specially designed for customer comfort, a
staff of discreet assistants and a carefully chosen stock of the latest fashions at
reasonable prices. After Wartski's death in 1965 the shop was acquired by Browns of
Chester, which in turn was taken over by Debenhams in 1976.

The Bull Inn shortly before the turn of the century. It was situated next door to the Albion, just above the Castle Hotel, at No. 162 High Street. The landlady was Mrs Ellen Williams, whose husband, John, and daughter, Elizabeth, are seen in the photograph. *Slater's Directory* of 1895 lists the Bull as one of 51 public houses in Bangor, 20 of which were situated in the High Street. The Bull was closed during the early 1930s and the premises occupied by the Royal & Legal Insurance Company.

The junction of Lôn Popdy and High Street during the 1920s. The premises occupied by Barclays Bank are reputed to have been the residence of the Dean of Bangor in 1450, and tradition has it that Owain Glyndŵr and his confederates met there to conspire against King Henry V. It became an inn around 1810, named the Blue Bell, demolished in 1880 and the City Hotel erected on the site. The confectioner's shop on the opposite corner was occupied by Mrs Mary Michael before being demolished in 1933 to make way for the Alliance Building.

A May Day procession winds its way up the High Street in 1912. Processions and parades were an important feature of town life during the Edwardian era and a popular form of entertainment which brought colour to an otherwise drab existence, particularly to the working class. They gave all age groups an excuse for dressing up and for civic dignitaries to show off their finery. The postcard was published by John Wickens, the well-known local photographer, as a souvenir of the occasion.

The British Hotel c.1905, with its private tennis court on the opposite side of the road, on what is now a garage forecourt. Tennis had become a popular pastime by the turn of the century and was taken up enthusiastically by women, although it is difficult to imagine how the lady in the photograph could possibly play athletically in a hat, a high-collared blouse and a long sweeping skirt. The British catered mainly for the more affluent visitors, where they could live in the style to which they were accustomed for three guineas a week.

A mounted detachment of the Royal Welsh Fusiliers parade outside the British Hotel in 1916 before being drafted to France, where one in every five who served there did not return. The sheer scale of the slaughter is difficult to imagine, with three-quarters of a million British servicemen killed and over two million injured. A quarter of a million had total or partial leg or arm amputations, while countless others suffered less visible disabilities, such as shell shock and gas poisoning, which remained with them for the rest of their lives.

The Arcadia 'picture palace' was the first cinema to be opened in Bangor (in 1910) and it provided a new experience of low-cost entertainment where the public could enjoy two or three hours of blissful escapism watching slapstick silent 'movies' of Charlie Chaplin and newsreels of national events, such as the FA Cup Final. But by 1934 the old wooden structure proved inadequate to cope with increased audiences so a new cinema (the Plaza), offering a high standard of comfort, was built in its place by J.R. Saronie.

The original station frontage on a postcard of 1909, with some of the portering staff waiting for the arrival of passengers. The appearance of the station was completely altered between 1924 and 1927 when a new building (the present one) was erected near the junction of Deiniol Road and Holyhead Road. The old frontage was retained on the up platform and an additional loop line constructed on the former forecourt. The parcels and luggage office, seen in the protruding section, was demolished and re-housed in the new building.

A view of the railway station in 1957, looking towards Belmont tunnel. The large engine sheds can be seen on the left of the photograph, with the up passenger loop line, now part of the present car park, on the right. During its heyday the station was a hive of activity, with its own goods yard, district engineer's headquarters, carriage sidings, wagon repair shed and motive power department, giving employment to over five hundred local men.

A nostalgic scene at Bangor station on a sunny afternoon in 1963 as a steam-hauled train prepares to pull away from the down platform. Two years later local trains sadly went over to diesel, and by 1968 all main line expresses had been converted as well. Rationalization of the railways during the mid-sixties had a disastrous effect on Bangor station, with the closure of most departments and a savage reduction in staff.

A panoramic view of Upper Bangor from Station Road in 1900. Deiniol Road had not yet been opened, and there was no development in the vicinity of the railway station until the large gravel pit was filled in during the early twenties and commercial properties erected on the site. St James' Church and the C & A Infirmary can be seen clearly, together with three substantial houses in Holyhead Road – Gwynfryn Villa, Fron Heulog (recently rebuilt) and The Rofft (now demolished).

A typical view of Deiniol Road in 1930, with a solitary car in the distance. Nowadays it is the busiest highway in Bangor. The road was opened from Love Lane to the railway station in 1904 and was widened during the late twenties in order to divert through traffic from the narrow High Street. But there is little evidence of this in the photograph as motorists still preferred to use the old route. The University Science Buildings were completed along Deiniol Road in 1926.

Workmen employed in the construction of the Sackville Road housing scheme in 1905.
This was Bangor's first venture into council house development, with nine units built in
Sackville Road and let at a rental of 7s. 6d a week, and a further thirty-four in Treflan
and Minafon to replace a number of slum dwellings demolished in Kyffin Square. The
new houses, which were built at an average cost of £176 each, had no bathrooms or
inside toilets, and tenants were not allowed to keep either dogs or lodgers.

A class of infants at St Paul's School in 1926. Built in 1858 as a Wesleyan denominational school for 620 children, it was one of eight schools in Bangor catering for children of infants and elementary age. Discipline was rigorous by modern standards, and so was parental control. Teaching was drearily factual, with emphasis placed on the repetitive learning of tables and rules of grammar, and one gains the impression from the photograph that school was tolerated rather than enjoyed, particularly by those of lesser ability.

The presence of a street photographer was still sufficiently unusual to attract the attention of the young man standing at the bottom of Glanrafon Hill in 1905 – a year after Deiniol Road had been opened through what was previously the Bishop's Park Estate. Prior to this, all horse-drawn traffic to and from Anglesey and Caernarfon had to proceed along the High Street. Three-storey houses were built on Glanrafon Hill in the 1850s, and many of them had been converted into lodging houses by the turn of the century.

This postcard view of the late 1930s has now completely changed. The University building is today all but obscured by the students' union and Theatre Gwynedd. Only the tower can now be seen from this location. The memorial was erected in 1923 in honour of the 220 Bangor men who had sacrificed their lives in 'the war to end all wars' – over one in five of all those who had enlisted. A further 95 names were later added to commemorate those who had fallen during the Second World War.

NEW CARNEGIE LIBRARY BANGOR.
OPENED BY LORD PENRHYN Nov 8th 07.

A generous gift of £2,500 from Andrew Carnegie, a wealthy American philanthropist, enabled the city council to build a new library in 1907. This replaced the old 'Free Library & Reading Room' which had been housed in cramped accommodation above Captain Jones's museum near the bottom of Lôn Popdy. An appeal was made to the public for books to add to the 4,000 transferred from the old library, and £250 was allocated for the purchase of new ones. Today, the library boasts a stock of over 36,000 books.

Members of the Bangor Fire Brigade pose for the camera on their new motor fire-engine, which had been purchased in 1926 to replace a horse-drawn one. The engine was housed in the town hall outbuildings until new headquarters were built in Union Street, behind the County Theatre, in 1943. The present fire station in Beach Road was opened in 1964. Bangor firemen were all part-time volunteers until the fire service was re-organised on a county basis in 1947, when full-time firemen were recruited for the first time.

The Royal Party arriving at the Bishops Palace, Bangor, July 1907.

A Royal occasion. King Edward VII's visit to Bangor on 11th July 1907 to lay the foundation stone of the new University College building. Still referred to as 'Bishop's Palace' by the publisher of this postcard, the building had been purchased by the city council from the Ecclesiastical Commissioners in 1902 together with the surrounding estate, through which Deiniol Road was opened two years later. In 1935 it was decided to demolish the old palace and to erect a new town hall on the site, but the plan was never implemented.

A large crowd gathers in Deiniol Road to watch a Union Jack tableaux performed by hundreds of schoolchildren in College Park on the occasion of Edward VII's visit on 11th July 1907. This postcard was one of a series published by Humphreys & Parry, the Bangor stationers, to record the many spectacular events of the day.

14th July 1911. King George V and Queen Mary meeting local dignitaries on the terrace of the University College after the official opening of the new building. Prince Edward, fresh from his investiture as Prince of Wales at Caernarfon the previous day, appears quite unconcerned as he chats to his sister, Princess Mary. Alongside the Royal children are Sir Harry Reichel, the College Principal, and Henry Hare, the architect. The building had been erected at a cost of £106,000 on land donated by the city council, and was financed largely by voluntary contributions.

Williams the
Central Book Mart
Bangor.

"HWFA MÔN"
Archdruid of Wales
Bangor National Eisteddfod
Gorsedd, 1902.

Hwfa Môn, the Archdruid, delivering his opening address at the Gorsedd Ceremony during the 1902 National Eisteddfod held in Bangor. A large pavilion, with seating for 8,000 and 'lit by electricity', was erected in Bishop's Park on a site opposite the present post office. Special trains brought in thousands of visitors, who were warned by numerous notices to 'beware of pickpockets'. The Eisteddfod was a financial success but was criticised in the local press for its 'excessive English character'. This postcard was published in 1905 to commemorate Hwfa Môn's lifelong contribution to the National Eisteddfod.

A class of infants at St Mary's National School, Garth Road c.1898, probably facing a camera for the first time in their lives. Compulsory education for all five to ten year olds was already well-established and had been free since the 'school pence' was abolished in 1891. St Mary's School was built in 1868 to accommodate 499 children, mainly from the densely populated Dean Street area. The re-organisation of elementary education in Bangor led to the closure of the school in 1968 and the building was converted into maisonettes.

Garth Road & Tabernacle Chapel, Bangor.

Little appears to have changed in Garth Road in ninety years, apart from the absence of traffic. Deserted roads were a normal feature of town life when this postcard was written in 1907 as the motor car was still a comparatively rare sight. This stretch of road was opened in 1834 and improved in 1902 in order to attract visitors to the pier. It was widened further in 1950 when Penuel Chapel was demolished. Garth Road was a desirable place to reside, and was much favoured by businessmen and professional people.

An early photograph, taken during the 1890s, showing a fine panoramic view of lower Bangor. The field between St Mary's Church and James Street, on what is now Maes-y-Dref, was the Bangor football ground, alongside which was Friars School, partly obscured by trees. The large open space beyond, extending as far as Hirael Bay, was part of the Friars Estate. Orme Road and Glynne Road had not been built, while Beach Road was largely undeveloped. The photograph also gives a clear perspective of the high density of housing in the Dean Street area.

A well-attended bazaar in the Drill Hall, Glynne Road, during the 1950s. The side stalls are manned by members of St Mary's Church, towards which the proceeds were donated. Bazaars and rummage sales were then the customary methods of raising money for various causes, but nowadays they appear to have been superseded by car boot sales. In addition to its military function, the Drill Hall was also let for Saturday night dances and boxing tournaments, and for use as a postal sorting office during the Christmas period.

ORME ROAD, BANGOR

Paradise lost. The only traffic seen in a peaceful Orme Road in 1911 are two bicycles and a horse-drawn coal wagon. It was not until the early thirties that the motor car started becoming a nuisance, and then only slowly, as it was gradually brought within the reach of the lower middle class. Compared with the tightly-packed, overcrowded dwellings in the working class district of central Hirael, Orme Road was a salubrious place to reside.

The innocence of childhood. A mixed class at Hirael Infants School in 1923, accompanied by their teacher, Miss Foulkes Jones. The building was opened in 1904, at a time when children could leave school at the age of twelve and seek work. It was not until 1918 that the school-leaving age was raised to fourteen. The children of the 1920s found their own ways of amusing themselves during out-of-school hours, whereas those of today expect entertainment to be provided for them.

A resident of Hirael on a postcard of 1910. Unfortunately he is unidentified, as the original owner has left no record of his name on the reverse side of the card – a common but irritating omission. Another puzzling feature is why he should have attracted the photographer's attention at all, as the poorer members of society were hardly ever photographed. His age is difficult to determine, but judging from his clothes it is likely that he was still working – probably at Port Penrhyn or in one of the Hirael slate yards – and he would have continued working as long as he could because the recently introduced old-age pension alone was insufficient to live on. Single persons over the age of seventy received five shillings a week and married couples seven shillings and sixpence. But for those too old or infirm to work, with no other resources and no children on whom to depend, there was no alternative but to seek the grudging help of the parish or to end their days in Glanadda Workhouse – the ultimate act of degradation.

The lower end of Ambrose Street shortly before the houses were demolished in the early seventies as part of the council's redevelopment programme. Built by speculators during the 1820s, the street was named after the Welsh poet William Ambrose (y Bardd Emrys) who was born in the Penrhyn Arms, where his father was the tenant. Ambrose Street was the hub of central Hirael and in 1895 it had as many as twelve shops and a sub-post office. During the 1930s some of its houses were sold for £150 each.

Beach Road in the late 1950s, almost completely devoid of traffic. The premises of David Cale, sailmaker and well-known Hirael character, can be seen clearly on the corner of Ambrose Street. The garage complex included a paint spraying shop and car hire business run by Thomas Richard Roberts. The entire block was demolished in the late sixties and a petrol filling station erected on the site. Foundry House, seen in the foreground at the junction with Foundry Street, was also demolished to make way for a tyre depot.

A mixed class of 34 children pose for their annual photograph at Garth School in 1920. W.R. Jones, seen on the right, spent 42 years at the school – 35 of them as headmaster – until his retirement in 1938. He was also an influential figure in the civic life of Bangor, being mayor for three consecutive years from 1928 to 1931. Owen Eames, on the left, also gave excellent service to the school – from 1903 to 1945 – and will be remembered by generations of children as a gifted teacher. The school was closed in 1968.

Garth Fields, the area between Ffordd Islwyn and the River Adda, and extending as far as the Crosville Garage, was converted into a recreational complex in 1933. Initially, three tennis courts were laid at a cost of £460 and the following year a further three courts were opened, together with a pavilion and changing room. Playing facilities were extended in 1938 with the laying of a large putting green. It was officially opened by Alderman W.R. Jones, seen on the left of the photograph alongside Dick Roberts, the attendant.

Hirael Bowling Club in 1956, a successful team which played in the Bangor & District League. The bowling green, along with the tennis courts and putting area, was lost to the town in 1965 when the indoor swimming baths were built on the site.

Standing (left to right)   Ted Jones, Seth Edwards, Tom Lewis, Arthur Jones, Hughie Griffiths, Idwal Roberts

Seated   Jack French, T.H. Jones, Ivor Hughes, Alderman Eirwyn Owen (Mayor of Bangor), Eddie Roberts, Hugh Owen

One of the fleet of 35 buses of Bangor Blue Motors Ltd, registered CC 7116, which entered service in 1927. The company was established in 1921 with a nominal capital of £2,000 and operated regular services to Caernarfon and Bethesda every fifteen minutes, to Beaumaris and Holyhead half-hourly, to Amlwch every hour and along five other routes less frequently. In 1928, in the face of fierce competition from rival operators, the company was sold to the Llandudno Coaching & Carriage Company, which in turn was taken over by Crosville Motor Services three years later.

The Bangor to Deiniolen bus, registered FR 8419, which was acquired by Crosville when UNU (You-Need-Us) Motor Services of Caernarfon was taken over in 1930, and it remained in service until 1938. This was one of over 50 buses operating from the Bangor depot, which was built in 1931 as the second largest in North Wales. Crosville expanded enormously during the thirties with the purchase of no fewer than 63 independent bus operators in North Wales, to give it a virtual monopoly of local passenger transport.

The first stage in the construction of the pier in 1894 – a time when pier-building mania had gripped the country and virtually every resort had one. It was built in order to attract more visitors to the town and to compete with Beaumaris and Menai Bridge for tourists disembarking from the Liverpool pleasure steamers. The pier was completed in May 1896 at a cost of £34,911, which included the purchase of Garth Ferry and the Gazelle Inn, and an average of 34,000 passengers landed there each summer up to 1914.

The pier in 1908, showing plenty of activity as one of the Liverpool pleasure steamers prepares to berth. The pier was a popular attraction for residents and visitors alike, who strolled its length to take the air and to see the ships arrive. Seasonal entertainment was also provided in the form of pierrots, concerts, brass bands, stunt diving and variety programmes performed by Will Summerson's Musical Middies. The ferry services were popular too, with the *Mona* plying to the Gazelle for a penny each way and the *Lady Magdalen* to Beaumaris for sixpence.

In December 1914 the cargo vessel *Christiana* was driven against the pier during a severe storm, demolishing some of the supporting pillars and 150 feet of the wooden deck. Temporary repairs, in the form of a narrow walkway, were carried out by the Royal Anglesey Engineers who at the time were being trained in the construction of pontoon bridges at Kingsbridge Camp, Llanfaes. The deck was finally rebuilt in 1921 but the pier never really recaptured the popularity of its pre-war days.

A leisurely stroll on the pier in the summer of 1914. These two ladies, although sadly unidentified, provide a clear picture of the fashions of the day, being conventionally clothed from neck to instep. Edwardian women would never be seen out of doors without a hat, even in summer, because of the widespread belief that the sun was harmful and that a tanned skin was a degrading feature in a woman. Clothing was relatively cheap. The mass production of ready-made garments brought prices tumbling down, and in the Wartski's sale of 1913 ladies coats were advertised for £2.2s, dresses from £1, lace blouses at 5s.6d and gloves from 1s.11d a pair. Before the First World War there was no equality of opportunity for women. The only jobs available to them were those which proved no threat to the career prospects of men, such as domestic service, dressmaking, nursing and infant teaching. Furthermore, they were not given the vote until 1918, and then only to those over the age of thirty who were ratepayers or the wives of ratepayers.

The *Clio* boys gather aboard for an impressive display in 1900. For over forty years the *Clio* was a familiar sight moored near the pier until she was broken up off the 'Ja Ja' jetty in 1920. She was an industrial training ship for 260 'homeless and poor respectable boys' between the ages of eleven and fifteen, and was regarded as the best source of recruitment for the mercantile marine, with technical instruction given in seamanship, signalling, gunnery, sailmaking, tailoring, shoemaking, carpentry and laundry work, as well as in the 'three Rs'.

The famous *Clio* boys' silver band on the pier in 1912. Along with the ship's bugle band it was always in great demand throughout the area for concerts, civic processions and fund-raising events. This postcard, which shows the *Clio* in the background, was one of a series produced by John Wickens of College Road.

The paddle steamer *Snowdon* approaching the pier in 1926. Built by Laird Bros at Birkenhead in 1892, she had a length of 175 feet, a speed of 14 knots and comfortable accommodation for 462 passengers. She plied daily each summer from Llandudno to Caernarfon, leaving at 10.30 am and calling at Beaumaris, Bangor and Menai Bridge, before arriving in Caernarfon at 1.00 pm. Occasionally she ventured further afield to Blackpool and the Isle of Man, as well as running excursions around Anglesey. She was broken up in 1931 and replaced by *St Seiriol.*

P.S. "LADY ORME.

The paddle steamer *Lady Orme* in 1935. Built in 1888 as the *Fuzilier*, she operated in Scottish waters until being acquired in 1935 by the Cambrian Shipping Company for summer excursions from Llandudno to Bangor and Menai Bridge. But this service generated little support because of competition from the more modern vessels, *St Tudno*, *St Seiriol* and *St Silio*. *Lady Orme* seemed bedevilled by a series of breakdowns, and throughout the 1938 season she was laid up in Hirael Bay before finally being broken up in October of the following year.

A crowded *St Seiriol* approaching the Menai Strait after the resumption of sailing in 1946. She was a familiar sight as she passed Bangor pier on her regular excursions around Anglesey. Built in 1931 to replace *St Elvies*, she was a smaller version of her sister ship, *St Tudno*. She was requisitioned by the Admiralty in 1939 and played a big part in the evacuation of Dunkirk, making several perilous voyages there through gunfire and aerial attacks. She made her final voyage on 6th September 1961 before being broken up at Ghent.

St Trillo off Bangor pier in 1950. She made her maiden voyage in 1930 as the *St Silio* but was re-named *St Trillo* on her return from minesweeping duties in 1946. Licensed to carry 568 passengers, she ran short excursions from Llandudno to Menai Bridge, as well as cruises to Amlwch. Her owners, the Liverpool & North Wales Steamship Company, went into voluntary liquidation in 1962 and *St Trillo* was sold to Townsend Ferries Ltd. She was chartered to P & A Campbell Ltd who continued to employ her on short cruises, but she was finally withdrawn from service in 1969.

Ice floes on the Menai Strait between the pier and the Gazelle Hotel during the severe cold spell of January 1963. Garth shore was frozen solid and miniature icebergs floated into Hirael Bay. No football was played for six consecutive Saturdays, and local leagues were forced to extend the season. But it was not as cold as the severe winter of 1947 when the one-mile expanse of the Menai Strait was frozen in places from bank to bank.

Enclosed Sea Bath, Bangor.

Siliwen open air baths in 1905. Sea bathing was popular with the Edwardians, who believed that it helped to cure a wide range of ailments. Surprisingly, Bangor was one of the first baths in the country to allow mixed bathing, whereas in other resorts it was strictly segregated, even up to 1910. From 1902 to 1914 an average of 8,000 people used the baths each year. The postcard shows that bathing costumes were all-enveloping, and it was not until the twenties that ladies' costumes became briefer.

Bangor, Menai Straits.

The Siliwen area in the early 1900s, a view now almost completely obscured by the Craig Menai apartments. Gorad Road, Hwfa Road and Buckley Road were largely undeveloped, and the only house visible is Trewern at the lower end of Craig-y-Don Road. There were a few houses in Siliwen Road (then called Menai Road), built in the early 1880s, which still retain their original names – Elm Bank, Bodafon, Bron Hwfa, and Menai Dale.

BANGOR. THE LOOKOUT.

The coachman was clearly confident that he would not meet any oncoming traffic as he drives around the bend on the wrong side of the road opposite the 'Lookout' in 1906. The motor car had not even begun to cause problems as it was still a novelty enjoyed by a mere handful of wealthy enthusiasts. Even as late as 1914 there were only 50 car owners in Bangor and just over 400 in the whole of Anglesey. The postcard was written by a holidaymaker who had visited the 'Lookout' from her lodgings in the Crescent.

The widening of Upper Garth Road in 1931, one of several road improvement schemes undertaken by the council in order to meet the increase in traffic during the early thirties, when the motor car was beginning to make an impact on people's lives. Motoring was no longer the prerogative of the well-to-do as a brand new Austin Seven could be acquired for as little as £120. Anyone over the age of seventeen could drive as there was no compulsory test until 1935, and then only for beginners.

University Hall, a hostel for women students in College Road, now re-named Neuadd Rathbone. Built in 1897 for £7,000, it replaced the former hostel at Bron Castell which closed after a widely publicised scandal. Discipline was harsh as Victorian puritanism was carried to the extreme. Residents were constantly under supervision by the warden, and unchaparoned women were forbidden to associate in private with men students, except on academic matters. This postcard was written in 1906 by a student at the hostel to a friend in Essex.

The ceremony of laying the memorial stone of the County School for Girls by Mrs Thomas Gee on 20th March 1897. The school had been established two years earlier in temporary premises in Horeb Chapel schoolroom, with 28 pupils under the headship of Miss M.J. Mason. Built of Ruabon red brick, the new school cost £2,320, much of it raised by private donations. It was formally opened on 9th October 1897, with accommodation for 100 girls, but further extensions increased its intake to 240 by the outbreak of the First World War.

The County School for Girls on a Wickens postcard six years after its opening. By the thirties progress was being hindered by a lack of space so in 1939 the school was moved to a new site in Ffriddoedd (the present Ysgol Tryfan), with places for 350 girls. The following year the old building was acquired by the University College to house the Museum of Welsh Antiquities until this was re-located in the old Canonry (its present home) in 1973. The former school now accommodates the University Music Department.

The pupils of Form 1 of the County School for Girls in 1926, resplendent in their new uniforms, with Miss Moseley, their form mistress and history teacher. School discipline was harsh, and a high standard of dress and decency was demanded. Pupils received an academic education on the basis that girls were as intellectually capable as boys. Entry at the age of eleven was selective, and those who failed to gain admission went to the Central School.

The message on this postcard, written in August 1905, indicates that this well-dressed family group was setting out for a week's holiday in Moelfre. The location is College Road, opposite the studio of John Wickens, who took the photograph. Before the emergence of the motor car and the bus, a slow uncomfortable journey by horse-drawn cab was the only means of transportation to a village untouched by the railway. The card was written by 'Lizzie' but the family is sadly unidentified.

The imposing Normal College (Coleg Normal) building around the turn of the century. The College was established in 1858, and during the first four years of its existence it was housed in Twrgwyn Chapel vestry until the new building was erected in 1862. With the increasing demand for teachers the College expanded, and in 1908 women were admitted for the first time. Two years later a large complex, including four halls of residence with accommodation for 200 students, was built on land adjoining the main building.

THE GEORGE HOTEL
BANGOR FERRY, BANGOR, N.W.

The George Hotel was built during the early 1770s and extended several times to cater for those travelling by coach to and from Ireland, and for the well-to-do who visited the area during the summer season. It was one of the most fashionable hotels on the entire length of the Holyhead Road, and among its more distinguished guests were Thomas Telford, Robert Stephenson and the Duke of Wellington. In 1919 the George was acquired by the Normal College as a hostel to accommodate the large influx of men students who returned after the war.

A mixed infants class at Cae Top School in 1904. The school was built in 1871 to house 150 elementary children and 120 infants. The headmaster from 1891 to 1923 was Herbert King, and the teacher in the photograph could well have been his wife, who was the infants mistress. Despite a great deal of poverty among the working class, the children look well-nourished and tidily dressed. Perhaps a special effort had been made for the occasion. The girls wear traditional pinafores, while some of the boys appear in Eton collars and clogs.

CYMDEITHAS GREFYDDOL, CAPEL TWRGWYN, BANGOR, N.W.

Twrgwyn Chapel was built in 1854 during the period when Upper Bangor was developing rapidly as a residential area for both the middle and working classes. Religion played an important part in people's lives during late Victorian and Edwardian times, and when this postcard was written in 1910 an estimated 72 per cent of the population of Bangor were chapelgoers, with a further 18 per cent attending church. Twrgwyn had a membership of 572 and its Sunday School boasted no fewer than 549 members, of whom 65 were teachers and officers.

Station Road, now named Holyhead Road, was a perfectly safe place for a young boy to walk in 1910 before motor transport completely disrupted town life. St James' Church was completed in 1866 at a cost of £4,000, much of it raised by private donations and house-to-house collections. Bangor's other parish churches – St Mary's and St David's – were built in 1864 and 1884 respectively. The horse-drawn cabs seen in the photograph were probably waiting to pick up fares from well-to-do churchgoers or visitors to the C & A Infirmary.

St James' Church choir pose for its annual photograph in 1929. The church was renowned for its choral music under the direction of R.J. Evans, organist and choirmaster from 1923 to 1963, who is seen in the centre of the back row. One of the choristers' chief 'perks' was the annual tea party provided in the church hall, a wooden structure erected on Glanrafon Hill in 1921, and known affectionately as 'Jimmy's' to generations of students and young Bangor people who attended the twice-weekly dances held there.

The official opening of a new wing of the C & A Infirmary by the Princess Royal on 14th July 1934. The extension housed two medical wards, a children's ward and an ophthalmic department, which raised the hospital's bed complement to 145. The cost of the new wing (£24,911) was financed by donations, gifts, bequests, annual subscriptions and various fund-raising schemes such as dances, fêtes and flag days. In 1948 the C & A was absorbed into the National Health Service so there was no longer a dependence on privately-raised capital.

The Princess Royal, daughter of King George V, at a fête to raise funds for the new wing of the C & A Infirmary prior to its official opening in July 1934. The fête, together with a grand ball, raised over £1,000 towards the building costs. The children in the photograph presented purses to the Princess, containing £200 collected towards the appeal. Note the nurses' long aprons, the lengths of which did not rise much until the late forties.

The first training group of nurses at the C & A Infirmary in 1938, with Miss Margaret Bonnell (matron) and Miss E.A. Davies (sister tutor). Probationary nurses had been recruited for many years but no formal teaching was provided until 1935, when the Infirmary was provisionally recognised by the General Nursing Council as a Training School. The following year it was given full recognition. The nurses, who were paid £2 per month whilst training, were accommodated in the former YMCA building on Glanrafon Hill, which had been converted into a nurses home in 1931.

The C & A Infirmary on a postcard written in 1935 by a patient to his mother in Amlwch requesting some apples on her next visit. During 1935 some 1,700 in-patients were admitted, each of whom spent an average of eighteen days in hospital, compared with fifty days in 1900. Patients were charged a fee for their maintenance but members of a Contributory Scheme, into which they paid 3d a week, entitled them to receive free treatment and maintenance. The scheme was discontinued in 1948 when hospital treatment was freed of all charges.

The annual Friars School photograph c.1910, with Mr Glynn Williams, Headmaster from 1879 to 1919, seated in the centre. The entire school consisted of only 111 boys, many of whom were boarders, and 7 members of staff. Class sizes were small so pupils were able to benefit from individual attention. Numbers increased after the First World War and extensions were added to the existing building, which had been erected in 1900 at a cost of £12,000.

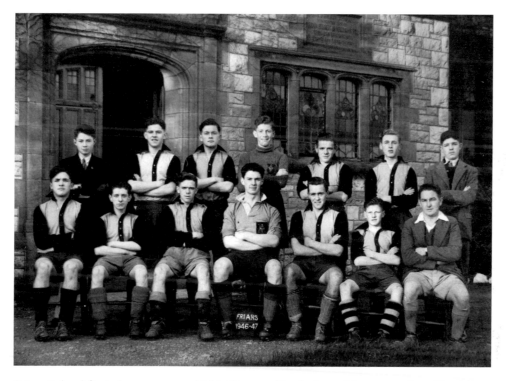

Friars School first eleven, season 1946-47, arguably the best side ever produced by Friars.
Five of the team later became professional footballers.

Standing (left to right) John Evans, Iorys Griffiths, Alun Jones, John Cowell,
Gwynfor Lewis, Charles Jones, Tom Bernard.

Seated Leslie Jones, Seth Edwards, Ken Lewis, Merfyn Roberts,
Gordon Lyon, John Merfyn Jones, Mr Edmund Humphreys.

The widening of Ffriddoedd Road in 1936. Private development at Belmont and the completion of the Maes Tryfan council estate had brought increased traffic along the dangerously narrow Ffriddoedd Road, so it was widened along its entire length at a cost of £19,000. Pavements were placed on both sides of the road, trees planted and walls built. The scheme took two years to complete as the roadmen had little more than pick and shovel to work with. Ffriddoedd Nurseries can be seen on the site now occupied by the Arfon Sports Hall.

The Technical College in the course of construction in 1955. A Technical Institute had been established eight years earlier in the former British Restaurant in Deiniol Road, but increasing demand for places on day-release and evening courses led to the building of a new college on five acres of land in Ffriddoedd. Large extensions, including a hall of residence, were later added in order to cater for a huge influx of full-time students.

Bryn Tawel Hill on a postcard of 1912. Originally this was the main thoroughfare from Bangor to Anglesey, so all horse-drawn traffic had to negotiate the steepness of Penchwintan Hill in order to reach the ferry near the George Hotel. But in 1816 Thomas Telford eased the difficulties of travellers and carriers by constructing a new road through Upper Bangor. The pair of cottages in the foreground have long since been demolished, while the road was closed to through traffic in 1995.

Staff and patients at Bodlondeb, a large house on the Menai Bridge Road owned by Henry Rees Davies, a member of the former ship-owning family. Whilst he was away on active service during the First World War the house was converted into a Red Cross Convalescent Hospital for wounded soldiers under the command of his sister-in-law, Mrs John Davies of Ceris. The nursing staff, as members of the Red Cross and of the local Women's Patriotic Guild, were all unpaid volunteers.

Eight motor cars pompously assembled for the photographer outside Treborth Hall c.1905, all owned by John Robert Davies of Ceris, his brother Henry Rees Davies and other members of their family. By 1912 they had no fewer than sixteen cars between them – almost a third of all those in Bangor. The Davies family had amassed a considerable fortune from their shipping business in Menai Bridge, and the ownership of a fleet of motor cars was the visible symbol of arrogant wealth.

A close-up view of the damage to EY 4, a 12 hp Wolseley owned by Samuel Chadwick of Llangoed, following an accident in October 1906. The car was being chauffeur-driven when it collided with the toll collector's booth on the Bangor side of the Menai Suspension Bridge, and the photograph shows the car being towed to nearby Ceris. Note the bald tyres, which were a normal feature on all early cars. Punctures were a constant problem on the untarred roads of the day, and tyres needed replacing every thousand miles or so.

Ainon Road Baptist Chapel in 1905, some twenty years before houses were built in Heol Dewi and Ainon Road. The building was erected in 1895, with seating for 300, and was one of 23 Welsh chapels in Bangor at that time. A Royal Commission Report of 1910 estimated that Ainon Road had 156 adherents, just under a half of whom were communicants, while the Sunday School had 60 members and no fewer than 10 teachers. Membership fell sharply after the Second World War and the chapel finally closed in the 1960s.

Bangor Railway Institute Boys Brigade c.1915. The movement was founded in 1883 and its militaristic guise captured the imagination of youngsters throughout the country, especially during the First World War. Part of its attraction was the opportunity to parade proudly through the town in uniform, led by the brigade band. The Bangor contingent, with over a hundred members between the ages of twelve and seventeen, was formed by railwaymen in order to encourage their sons to develop a sense of loyalty and self-discipline, and to prepare older boys for military training.

E. ROBERTS   J. HUGHES. BILLY   R.V.J. JONES

Three former Bangor railwaymen pose for the camera as proud recruits in the Royal Garrison Artillery before sailing to the killing fields of France. They were some of the hundreds of young Bangor men who, in a surge of patriotism, had volunteered to fight 'for King and Country' before conscription was introduced in 1916 in order to replace the vast numbers lost in the earlier battles of the war.

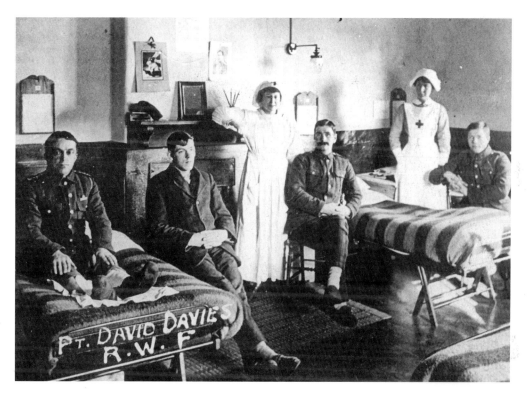

Private David Davies, an ex-Bangor railwayman who had enlisted in the Royal Welsh Fusiliers during the First World War, convalescing with fellow servicemen in the County Hospital after being wounded in France. The hospital was built in 1914 as a Poor Law Infirmary to replace the old workhouse in Caernarfon Road, but shortly afterwards it was requisitioned for use as a military hospital before becoming a County Hospital in 1930. When management passed to the National Health Service the hospital was re-named St David's.

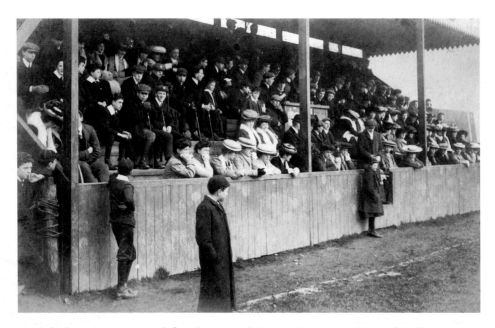

A packed spectators' stand for the annual University versus Normal College soccer match in 1907. The venue was the Bangor football ground, then located at Maes-y-Dref, before the field was converted into allotments in 1919 and built upon seven years later. Fashions contrast sharply with those of today. The women students support large hats and all the men wear cloth caps, while a handful of Friars boys are seen in starched Eton collars, knickerbockers and school caps.

A break between events at the amateur athletic sports held on the Bangor cricket field at Farrar Road (now the football ground) on Whit Monday 1908. This annual event attracted large crowds, and special cheap day tickets were issued by the railway company from as far afield as Chester. Although Edwardian athletes were poorly equipped and uncoached, they achieved some remarkable performances and provided great entertainment. This postcard is one of a series produced by John Wickens to record the various track and field events held during the day.

Bangor Red Star Football Club, season 1905-06, one of a dozen amateur teams in Bangor at that time. Football was an exciting spectator sport which received enthusiastic support from men who had little else to occupy their Saturday afternoons, and to whom other sports seemed dull in comparison. Above all it was entertaining, with the emphasis always on attack, and the forwards playing in a line-of-five. The safety first 4-4-2 and other defensive formations were reserved for a future generation.

Bangor Football Club, season 1922-23.

Back row (left to right)	D.J. Thompson, S. Rathbone, H. Lock.
Middle row	R.R. Roberts (groundsman), A Kortegas, J. Price Jones, R.E. Jones, J. Lewis, R. Owen (chairman), D. Burns (treasurer).
Seated	H.O. Williams (secretary), T. Lewis, J.O. Jones, N.H. Lewis, R. Lock, M. Pattison, H. Jones (trainer).

Bangor Rugby Club, season 1931-32. The Club was re-formed in 1930 after a lapse of over fifty years, and during the thirties it had a succession of temporary homes – at Ffriddoedd, in Penrhyn Park and on the cricket field at Ty Newydd. Although soccer was the dominant sport in Bangor, rugby was played at the University and Normal Colleges, as well as at Friars. The school had switched from association football to rugby in 1919 but reverted back to soccer with the appointment of Ivor Williams as headmaster in 1935.

SIR CHARLES THANKS JERRY M.
JERRY M. SMILES

Jerry M's triumphant return to Vaynol after winning the Grand National in 1912. Sir Charles Assheton-Smith, its owner, enjoyed a remarkable hat-trick of Grand National successes with *Covercoat* in 1913 and *Sunlock* the following year. Although horse-racing was largely the preserve of the well-to-do, results were avidly followed by the working class as off-course betting was a popular pastime in the public houses, with stakes of little more than 'sixpence each way'. The other form of national gambling – the football pools – did not arrive until the twenties.

Blanche at Port Penrhyn in 1947. Built by Hunslet of Leeds in 1893 and named after the wife of Edward Sholto Douglas-Pennant, the third Baron Penrhyn, *Blanche* was used for hauling slates from the quarry to the port for shipment to distant markets. She also hauled the quarrymen's train which took the Bangor men to Bethesda each morning and returned them after work. In 1963, after seventy years' service on the line, *Blanche* was sold to the Festiniog Railway Company, along with her sister locomotive *Linda*.

Loaded slate wagons, hauled by *Blanche*, en route to Port Penrhyn near the halfway passing loop on 'lein bach'. She normally hauled up to thirty wagons on the journey to the quay, with each wagon capable of carrying two tons of slate. A decline in the slate industry, together with rising maintenance costs and increased competition from road transport, led to the closure of the railway in 1962. The track was lifted three years later.

The slate ship *Sybil Mary*, a steamer of 270 gross tons, was built for Lord Penrhyn in 1921 to add to his existing fleet of ships used for carrying slates from the quay to British and Continental ports. After the Second World War Port Penrhyn declined in importance as most of the quarry's production went by road and rail. Only one shipment by sea took place so *Sybil Mary* was sold before being broken up at Dublin in 1951.

Pandora was the smallest vessel in the Penrhyn fleet of slate ships, having a gross tonnage of 203. She was built at Wallsend in 1892 and acquired eleven years later to supplement the cargo capacity of *Mary B. Mitchell*, *Harrier*, *Bangor*, *Pennant* and *Penrhyn*. *Pandora* was sold to the Ministry of Transport in 1947, and four years later she floundered in a gale off Whitby with all hands lost.

The University College housed in its temporary premises in the former Penrhyn Arms Hotel in 1910. Bangor had been selected as the site for the college in 1883 amid strong claims by twelve other towns in North Wales, and it opened its doors the following year with an intake of 58 students. The building was demolished in 1933 to make way for a new road, but its porch can still be seen today on the eastern approach to Bangor as a reminder of the building's former glory.

A Bangor council road gang pose briefly for the camera before the outbreak of the First World War. Roadmen were shamefully exploited by their employers. In 1914 they earned a mere 4d an hour for a 55-hour week, which represented starvation wages of 18s a week, but by working up to 12 hours a day earnings could be increased to £1. Yet even this was less than enough to maintain a family of four in basic necessities at a time when living standards were being eroded by inflation.

The completion of Ffordd-y-Castell, Maesgeirchen, in December 1937, shortly after the first tenants had moved in. A total of 304 houses were built on the estate before the outbreak of war as part of the council's redevelopment programme to rehouse families from condemned and overcrowded properties in the town. The houses were constructed at an average cost of £390 each, and tenants were charged a rent of 7s.6d a week. After the war a further 274 houses and flats were built on the estate, plus 234 at Tan-y-Bryn.

An early photograph of Melin Esgob (Bishop's Mill), a watermill for grinding corn into flour, situated on the banks of the River Cegin alongside 'lein bach', about a mile from Port Penrhyn. Possibly dating from the middle ages, the mill was owned by the Bishop of Bangor and leased to various tenants before being sold to Lord Penrhyn in 1862. The mill continued to work until the last quarter of the nineteenth century, but once cheap grain started flooding into the country it fell into disuse and the buildings were demolished.

The model village of Llandegai on a Wickens postcard of 1928. It was built by Lord Penrhyn for his estate workers at the end of the eighteenth century with the stipulation that 'no corrupting alehouse' could be opened there.

Felin Hen station on the outskirts of Bangor, situated on the Bethesda branch line, a four-mile single track with a gradient of 1 in 40. It was opened in 1884, and during its heyday in the 1930s no fewer than 32 trains stopped at Felin Hen each weekday, 16 in each direction, with additional ones on Saturdays. The third class return fare to Bangor was 6d. The station was closed with the withdrawal of passenger services in 1951, but the line continued to cater for goods traffic until complete closure in 1963.